Jump-Start Guide
for Independent Publishing

Jump-Start Guide
for Independent Publishing
Entrepreneurial First Step Guide

Entrepreneurial First Step Guide
Margaret Cook, M.Ed., L.P.C.
Licensed Professional Counselor
Life Coach
Book Coach

Published by All She Writ Publishing, LLC
P.O. Box 1193
Maryland Heights, MO 63043

ISBN-10: 0988690225
ISBN-13: 978-0-9886902-2-6

Cook, Margaret
Beginners' guide to publishing books and articles
independently and affordably.

Table of Contents

Skill Assessment

You have a message to share. You want to write a book or you have a book that you have written. You selected this jump-start guide to get a few ideas about how to independently publish your writing.

The best place to start is taking stock of your own skills. Take a sheet of paper or sit down at your computer to make a few lists. This exercise is a nice reality check. Be honest, but not too humble. Be realistic in your honesty.

Take a few minutes to think about writing and publishing a book. Make four columns on your page:

1. I am great at (so great that I could teach or help others)...
2. I am good at or good at learning how to ...
3. I am really weak and need help with...
4. I know that I will need to hire help for (beyond my skills)...

Keep this list handy. As you read this book, make changes to your list. As you find out things that are involved with writing and publishing a book, you will want to enter the skill in the column that best describes your skill level.

Basic Business

Consider the reason you picked up this book. You wanted to write a bestseller. You wanted to get your message out to the world. You wanted to see if you could write a book. Go ahead; make your list of why you are reading this guide:

_____

_____

_____

In your reasons, or in addition, this guide will help you understand the basic business of book writing and publishing. The bottom line (pun intended) of any business endeavor is to create a positive cash flow. The successful business produces more income than the expenses associated with the endeavor. In my experience as an entrepreneur and through providing coaching and counseling services for more than two decades, I have worked with many people. I found it particularly common for people who have been in debt to take on a "business" attempting to earn extra money. In most instances, the attempt COST money and did not produce adequate income to break-even. I wrote the *Jump-Start Guide for a Start-Up Online Business* in response to this concern.

I have been working with writers and authors since the 1990s. Those early years centered around helping people understand their writing process and getting their work published in traditional publishing methods. In the last ten years, the writing process may have become a little easier because of technology. However, getting books published now has several possibilities that are different from traditional publishing. In considering the best way to publish, the writer needs to be informed so that s/he is able to make good decisions. This *Jump-Start Guide for Independent Publishing* will give an overview of the information that will help the writer view the decision from a basic business model. The model offers careful consideration to keeping costs/expenses in control to assure the prospect of profitability.

Online Income

Technology makes modern writing and publishing easier than it has ever been before. This guide will focus on the sale of books using online tools. The guide is a quick overview. It will help you, the reader, make choices about publishing and selling books. You will likely need to do further research on the particular methods you select for publication and sales.

The internet is brimming with ideas, services and information products to help people write, publish and market books. As with most information on the internet, consider the source and the reputation of the website. At the early stage of your business as a writer/publisher, be very conscious of the possible costs of these services and products. The more you spend on services or products, the higher your costs for your book and the more books you have to sell before you can make a profit.

You will also find the internet affords you a number of ways to promote your book, sell your book and related products, and produce income. This guide will focus on keeping expenses low and finding/developing ways to increase income.

Create a Budget for the Best Publishing Model

Budgeting is an age-old method for planning expenditures and staying within the constraints of income. Business planning involves a clear-eyed, fact-based approach to money. This is especially true when it relates to writing a book. Your book is a labor of love. It involves a high level of emotional commitment and a remarkable ego investment. This can easily wreak havoc on the best attempts to budget.

Building an accurate budget will require that you know how you will go about publishing your book. Refer back to the skill assessment that you did in the first chapter. We will explore four general models. You need to know how much money you have to work with as an investment. Within the constraints of that sum, you will have to determine what you will be able to learn to do yourself and what services you will need to hire/buy. You will want to concentrate your investment resources on the aspects of your book that are most likely to pay off quickly.

One example of publishing is the vanity press model that was the historical root of independent publishing. The vanity publisher would extract a healthy fee from the author in exchange for publishing a book. Authors would pay relatively large sums of money to see their books in print. The vanity press publishers continue to this day. They are sometimes called author services, or some are called publishers. The main difference between a traditional publisher and a vanity press is that the costs associated with publication are paid by the author when the publisher uses a vanity press model.

As you prepare your book for publication, you may want to think about what assistance will make your book successful. You will be better off purchasing some services to assure the high quality of your book and to reduce the number of things you have to do yourself. The vanity press model may give you the opportunity to have one-stop shopping and the support of someone to guide you through the entire process of publishing a book. I recently met with a first-time author. She was considering a contract with a University Press that offered a model where she would pay for the book publication, and the University Press would coordinate the pre-publication services (editing, proofreading, design, printing, etc.) You may want to prepare for "sticker shock" when you hear the costs of some of the programs. Most vanity presses now have several packages of services to offer the author a choice of expenditures. Think of this model as full-service when money is no object. The disadvantage for the vanity press model is that it tends to be expensive.

The internet is also brimming with coaches and programs for authors. These services offer to teach or guide authors through the process that is described as "Do It Yourself (DIY)." Many of these programs are digital, online classes or live conferences. Participants may also have the opportunity to purchase additional author services á la carte. The service providers may offer book covers, marketing, proofreading, templates for interior design and a variety of online tools for additional fees. The main drawback for this model is that the costs tend to spiral upward with subtle pressure to continue spending.

The current traditional publishing market is also an expensive adventure for many authors. A traditional publisher will expect the author to pay for any permissions, bear some costs of promotion and possibly cover expenses related to travel and events. In the traditional publishing model, an author will usually contract with an agent who works to locate a publisher. The agent and the publisher will be paid from the proceeds of your book. They will want reasonable assurance that you will be a profitable writer. The writer gets a royalty (a percentage) for every book that sells. The publisher may pay you an "advance" on your book. The advance is a payment the publisher makes against future royalties. Some contracts with publishers now make the advance repayable to the publisher if you do not sell enough books to earn the advanced royalties. Some studies report that more than half of the books published under the traditional model never earn back the advance. Some traditional publishers are also offering contracts that have no advance and sometimes have an improved royalty percentage to compensate for this. In a later chapter we will review some of the advantages and disadvantages of various publishing models. The point in this chapter is that there are expenses associated with traditional publishing for the author. The publisher will usually provide the editing, proofreading, cover, interior design and general marketing.

The book publishing industry has experienced a transformation because of technology. Digital printing has made it affordable to print a small number of books or just one copy at a time. This has become the Print on Demand (POD) model. The printing is typically done through Lightning Source. Because some aspects of using Lightning Source could be complicated for anyone inexperienced, a host of other providers offer more customer support and services [i.e., Lulu, BookBaby, Create Space (Amazon affiliated), etc.] In addition to printing the book, the POD service will offer to sell services to the author. Some of the services will be very affordable or free if you are publishing with them. The International Standard Book Number (ISBN) is a good example of this. The POD service may offer to include an ISBN number for free. The free ISBN is usually registered to the POD publisher. The POD publisher may also offer you an option to purchase an ISBN that would be registered to you for a nominal fee. You may also purchase ISBN numbers directly from Bowker (ISBN.org). Bowker will sell individual ISBNs or blocks of ISBNs that are numbered sequentially. You may want to purchase numbers directly from Bowker if you will have a book in several formats, and you want the numbers to be sequential. For most first-time authors/publishers the free or low cost ISBN will be adequate.

If you publish on Amazon's Create Space, the free ISBN will show Create Space as the publisher. Having the low-cost ISBN registered to your own publishing company is preferable.

In addition to the advent of POD, the transforming technology now brings electronic (eBooks) to the market. Readers access the eBook using a computer, tablet, eReader device or smart phone. Since the eBook eReaders are proprietary, the eBook format is specific to the brand of the eReader. Apple uses the iBook platform, Barnes and Noble has the Nook, and Amazon has the Kindle. There are a few other eBook readers that use a generic eBook format (EPub is most common). Each eBook reader uses a different type of file. When you publish a book, you have to format it specifically for the different eBook readers. There is also a format for iBooks that is mostly template based. The eBook market is growing rapidly. Although the formatting can be a little challenging, the production of an eBook is the least expensive way to publish a book currently. The publication process can go very quickly. Making changes or updates to the files after you have published your eBook is relatively easy. If you have full color photographs in your book, the eBook will be drastically more affordable than a full color print book. As you become more advanced in your formatting skills, you may even want to include various types of media in your eBook. Be aware that a large eBook file could have expenses related to the download/delivery that you would pay. If you are doing a media-rich eBook, do some research into managing the file size to contain the costs. Some formats do not have a cost associated with delivering the file. A media-rich book may be more successful on a platform without the associated file delivery expenses.

Consider hiring help formatting your eBook inexpensively on micro job sites like Fiverr.com or oDesk.com even if you are pretty good with technology. If you are very limited in your technology skills, invest in a reputable provider that specializes in formatting. You may find providers through search engines or the Kindle Direct Publishing (KDP) Conversion Resources. If you know that you are planning to initially do BOTH an eBook and a paperback, you may want to do the paperback first through Create Space and have them do the Kindle conversion. The Create Space site indicates that they will do the file conversion for $69. (That is the information on pricing at the time this book is going to press. Please check for current information when you are ready to publish.)

Considering the four models that I just described: 1. Vanity Press 2. Traditional Publishing 3. Print on Demand or 4. eBook publishing, you will want to decide which model will best meet your needs. Do some research online, talk to people who have used the services and, by all means, read the fine print of anything you decide to do before you pay any money. There is no substitute for due diligence. You probably will not become a best-selling author. You might, but it doesn't happen to a large number of people. Be wary of programs that make it sound like everyone becomes a celebrity.

Here is a quick summary of the choices I have discussed:

Model	Advantage	Disadvantage	Notes
Vanity Press	• Lots of customer support	• High cost • Customer support is not necessarily customized	
Traditional Publishing	• More prestige • Much of the work/expense handled by the publisher	• Difficult to get accepted • Timeline to publication may be several years	
Print On Demand	• Relatively Inexpensive • Quick timeline to publication	• Much to learn • Many decisions	
eBook Publication	• Very low costs (least expensive) • Easy to make updates or changes • Fast timeline to publication	• Formatting challenges • Multiple formats may be necessary	

Make your own list that reflects your skills and weaknesses. Be as honest as possible. Don't be afraid to do some research and estimate some costs.

Remember that every expense will contribute to the cost associated with your book. The more you spend, the more books you will need to sell to recover your costs and the longer it will take to turn a profit. This is why a very good budget is important. Once you establish a budget, you will need to work hard to stay in the budget. You may need to plan some margin for error the first time you publish a book.

Let's consider starting with the least expensive and most learning intensive publication model. The advantage here is that you will learn about everything that goes into publishing a book, you will be in control of the process, and, most of all, you will be able to manage the costs. Consider publishing first in an eBook format. There are very few costs associated with publishing eBooks. A very strong business model would lead with the eBook until the sales produced enough profit to pay for publishing the paperback (or hardback) book.

The costs associated with the eBook will minimally include: editing assistance, cover design, ISBN expenses, formatting expenses, permissions fees, expenses for obtaining reviews/testimonials, marketing materials and a reasonable investment of your own time to develop the skills and accomplish the publishing tasks.

In addition to the costs associated directly with the book, you will also need to budget for marketing your eBook. Take a few minutes to brainstorm any of the costs you know you will incur in this area. If you do not already have a website, you should plan this marketing expense sooner rather than later. You may also need marketing materials like postcards, bookmarks, business cards and flyers. You will need to obtain or write press/media releases, and you may need professional photographs of yourself and stock photos for your cover or other marketing venues.

Budget Worksheet

Enter all of the information categories and estimated expenses for each in a spreadsheet. Keep a running total and keep track of the actual expenses in addition to the ones you are estimating now. Just like the household budget, if one expense goes over, you will want to make another expense come in under the estimate. Comparison shop all of the services (items on the budget). As you shop and compare, you will learn about the service and the typical rates. This will help you negotiate for services and also obtain the best value for your investment.

When you have the total, compare it to the money that you honestly have to invest. If you do not make this money back, can you afford to spend it without return? If the number is too high, do some more research and see where you may be able to cut costs. Make sure the initial investment is within your means. If not, consider postponing the book project until you have the money. Some authors pre-sell paperbacks to raise the funds. That may or may not work for you, so approach this model carefully.

The total expenditure should help you set the price for your book. If you are publishing an eBook first, look at the other eBooks in your market. What are they typically selling for on the platform you will use? I publish my books on Amazon through Kindle Direct Publishing (KDP) for the Kindle eBook, and I publish the paperbacks using Create Space. I determine the price of my book by looking at my costs and the other books in the market. If you contain the costs on the eBook, you may be able to price your book between $2.99 – $8.99. Shorter books will attract more buyers at the lower price point. The more valuable your material is, the more you will be able to charge.

Determine the price for your paperback by looking at the other books that are similar to your book. Then, look at the information on Create Space concerning your likely cost per copy. If you have a lean budget for your book, you may be able to price your book at 2.5 times the cost per copy you will pay. (For example, if your cost per copy is $2.50, your retail price could be $6.25.) If your budget involves some significant expenses and it would be difficult to break-even at that price point, consider setting the retail price based on the comparable books in the market. If you price your book too high, some readers will not take a chance on an unknown author. If your price seems too low compared to other titles in the genre, the potential buyer may not believe that your book is valuable or worth much. Doing some market research can pay off if you look at the information on Amazon and in your local bookstores. Amazon gives you suggestions from "people who viewed this." This may help you identify the other books in your genre.

Using the price you just decided, calculate the amount you will make on the platform you will use for publishing (i.e., Amazon Kindle, iBooks, Nook, etc.) Take the amount you will make per book (this is less than the sale price) and divide it into the total on your budget worksheet. Total budget ÷ payment per book = the number of books you will need to sell to break-even. How confident do you feel that you will be able to sell that number of books? Work with the numbers until you have a break-even point that seems realistic. Reduce the expenditures or increase the price until you have a number you feel sure you can obtain.

Writing

There are excellent resources on the market and on the internet to help you as a writer. Consider what makes good writing. Some resources can inspire you to make your book the best. Remember that you are writing for an audience. Keep that audience in mind as you write. Test your material on people who are like your audience. When I was writing this book, I happened to meet four writers who were writing and publishing their first books. I invited all of them to call in for a weekly teleclass. They helped me understand what information they needed. I was able to use the material in this book to help guide them. I developed the book based on my experiences with the books I have published and with the authors that I have coached. Many writers meet regularly with a writers' group. Sharing your writing in a group can improve your writing exponentially.

Writing well involves considerable attention to revising, editing and proofreading. Using the services of a professional editor may be a very wise investment for a first-time author. An editor will help you improve the structure and the message of your book. A well-edited book is noticeable. If at all possible, make the investment in having your book edited. You may also need help with the proofreading. The more I look at things I have written, the more errors I find. Sometimes I look past errors because I become too familiar with what I have written. Always have a few people who can help you proofread. Proofreading is particularly important if you are publishing a paperback/print version of your book. Printed books have a long shelf life and making changes once the files are uploaded costs money. You will manage your budget more effectively if you are conscientious about proofreading and ordering proof copies (more than once) before releasing your print version for publication.

The eBook format has a distinct advantage. It is fairly easy and free to make corrections and upload the new eBook files. Amazon will even notify buyers that you have an updated file for them to download. This courtesy notification from Amazon will help remind your audience about your book. If you make substantial changes in a file, you may want to consider making it a subsequent edition. However, if the general content is not significantly altered, you may not need a subsequent edition. Each edition must have its own ISBN number. An update/revision of an existing edition uses the same ISBN. You would ordinarily remove (deactivate) the prior edition of the eBook when the new edition comes out. If you are in a field that is rapidly changing, eBooks may be the best way to publish.

Most writers use the word processing software with which they are most familiar. Because you may attempt to do your own formatting, I can offer a few time-saving tips. When typing your document, do not do any formatting when writing. Try not to add any bold type, italics or other special features. Use 12 point type in a standard font (i.e. Times Roman). Your writing will include only paragraphs, punctuation and words. When you have finished all of the writing, run the spell check and make corrections to spelling and grammar. Save this file. Now copy the entire document and paste it onto the notepad (program under accessories on a PC). This will "strip" any code snippets that you created in the course of your writing. Copy the entire text on the notepad and paste it into a NEW DOCUMENT in your word processor. This is the copy where you will format the text for your eBook.

Formatting Tips

The eBook will not have page numbers. Do not add page numbers, headers, footers, watermarks or other formatting characteristics that you will not have in the eBook. If you have pictures, tables, charts, figures or graphics, you must scan them and insert the JPEG image (centered) in the correct place in the text. The scanned image dots per inch (dpi) should be at least 300dpi. I will talk more about that later. The JPEG is best set at 500 X 700 pixels and make it 100% scale in Word. Press Enter twice before you insert the picture and twice after it is inserted to help it float well on the screen from the text. Make sure that you INSERT the image. DO NOT copy and paste it into the document.

Look at a few eBooks, and you will see that they frequently have a blank line between the paragraphs OR an indentation of the first line of the paragraph. You may select whichever you prefer, but do not do BOTH. You will want to INSERT a page break at the end of each chapter. The Kindle formatting program will automatically create a paragraph based on your format. Search and read about formatting books for Kindle (or whatever platform you are using). Look for reputable sources and current information. The formatting processes continue to improve. Getting the most recent tips will be a good use of your research time.

The Table of Contents (TOC) is the most important navigation tool of an eBook for your reader. This is sometimes the most unfamiliar part of the formatting process. Because an eBook does not use page numbering, the reader moves to the parts of the book needed by using the hyperlinks in the TOC. Use meaningful chapter titles. The reader will have problems finding information if the chapters are called "Chapter 1..." There are basically two ways to create a table of contents. Select the one that seems most intuitive for you. Use only one method and don't switch back and forth within the same book/file.

Method one involves the internal word processor method of creating the table of contents. The drawback here is that it tends to have a lot of strange things that happen in translation to the eBook format. I confess that I have used this method and found myself ready to pull my hair out in the Kindle formatting practice. I offer my great thanks to the Fiverr. com pros who helped me with formatting in my first books. I learned that a better (though more time consuming) second method involves bookmarking and inserting hyperlinks manually.

I am not an expert at this. I am not a very technical computer user. I included a summary of this method for you at the back of the book. I suggest that you review it, try it, do some additional research for easier ways, or decide if this is something you will need to hire help to do. If you know you are hiring help for this, just skip this section of the book. This might make your eyes cross or your head hurt if technology is a source of stress for you.

Idea Inventory

If you are like many would be writers, you struggle with identifying what you will write about. I want to encourage you to take a risk and write. Write something that you know. Remember when we did the skill assessment at the beginning of the book? Write about the things that you identified as strengths. These are the topics where you could help or teach someone else. Not everyone starts with non-fiction, but it can be an easier place to learn the process of independently publishing. You need to gain some experience with writing and publishing. Consider writing something that is relatively short. That can make learning the formatting process much easier.

In the past few years, I have also helped a number of writers convert their original research and/or important papers they wrote in school that would have relevance and a timely impact for a niche or group of people. If you have written a number of things in the past, look at what you have written and think about updating or expanding something that you identify as particularly relevant and helpful for an audience you would like to reach. Writing that sells is not writing that is about you. It is writing that meets a need that the readers believe they have.

Develop your idea inventory from the skill assessment. Make a list and add to it the ideas that you feel you have some expertise to share. A narrow topic where you have a depth of knowledge is usually easier to write about. However, some writers identify a specific need and then do the research. Writing a "how to" book where you (the writer) are learning along with the reader could make the topic more approachable. This might also help you think clearly about how to organize the new information and will help you learn more from your research. Select a topic that you need to research and develop the ideas based on your need to know.

My idea for this book developed from a presentation that I outlined based on questions people asked me about publishing books and how much they should be spending. I realized that the audience was being conditioned to spend a lot of money with a "hope" of making it big and becoming rich. It was the frequent story of good people spending money they could not afford because of an emotional need to believe that when they bought this "too good to be true" package they would soar to celebrity status. My inbox is full of these offers. For a few hundred up to a few thousand dollars a program, seminar, online course, vanity press, etc. will make the purchaser a successful author. I listen to most of the free content they offer inviting people to buy the course/services. I am well aware of the great marketing and affiliate relationships that people create so that they are able to make money from would be authors/publishers. I enjoy many of the free presentations, but I do not buy the programs. It would drive the cost of my books up to a level of expense that I would not want to have the pressure to recoup. These are buyer-beware stories. I encourage due diligence and careful budgeting as a part of starting any small business. Do I spend money to make money? Yes, but not more than reasonably fits in the budget for the project. I have taken classes locally at the community college on software. I have paid for assistance with aspects of publishing. I hire an artist for book covers, marketing materials, logos, and other features of the process that require expertise. I have also invested in some books to learn how to do some of the technical processes that I felt I could learn. I shop carefully and keep the costs in mind with every expenditure.

In 2007, I joined a local group for publishing, the St. Louis Publishers Association (SLPA). The annual membership fees afford me an opportunity to learn a good deal, locate good resource materials, find local vendors and help fellow writers with the process. If you have a local organization like this, the dues may be a very worthwhile expenditure for the learning and the contacts. Writing can be a lonely profession and having a regular opportunity to meet with other writers can be a nice source of enrichment.

Key Words

Every modern writer needs some proficiency for identifying the key words that users are putting in search engines. Using key words in book titles, book descriptions, websites and promotional material will increase the discoverability of your book.

You may already be familiar with some of the tools for key word research. I will give a few examples. Again, I tend to use free tools rather than paid resources that increase costs. The disadvantage of this is that some of the key word search tools that are free limit the number of times you can use them, and they tend to vanish frequently from the internet landscape. You may have to do a little research when you are ready to find some of the current, free key word search tools.

https://freekeywords.wordtracker.com/

http://www.wordstream.com/key words

https://adwords.google.com/ - it appears that Google is now using a planner tool that requires an ad account

http://www.semrush.com/

http://www.quintura.com/ -This is not actually a key word tool, but it can help you see related words. See also tools like http://ubersuggest.org/

http://www.google.com/trends/ -This is not a key word tool, but it shows the searches over time.

Using your idea list from this chapter and the last one, try to find about 10 key words that are associated with your best writing idea or topic. Keep this list handy. Look actively for ways to use these terms in your book title, descriptions and website.

Book Titles

The title of a book is the most powerful tool for attracting the reader. A clever title that does not contain key words or an adequate description may go completely unfound by the intended audience. Brainstorm a dozen titles for your book and make sure they all contain some key words.

Get audience input by asking people you know to "vote" for the title they think is most effective. You want a title that garners attention and that is descriptive enough. Many books make good use of having a title that includes a more descriptive subtitle. If you already have a website or social media site with a good amount of traffic, you may be able to set up an online poll for letting prospective readers vote on the possible titles. Doing this when you have a dozen working titles will not work very well. However, having the election of the best title from the top three would be great. You could offer to hold a drawing to give the winning voter a free copy of the book when it is published.

Categorically Speaking

The key words help readers find your book. A key word rich title and book description are the best tools for connecting with your audience. You will also need to identify a category for your book. Amazon sorts books by standard classifications. Look up the Book Industry Standards and Communications Category (BISAC) listing. You will also want to look at how books are organized on Amazon. Try to select meaningful categories for your reader and categories that are not as "full" of titles. Being in a category with fewer books might help you achieve a higher sales ranking on Amazon.

Websites and Social Networks

In your skill assessment, you may have indicated that you would need help with technology. This chapter is one of the more technologically challenging aspects of publishing your book. In addition to having your book available online somewhere (e.g., Amazon), you will need to have places online where you can provide information and connect with your readers.

Amazon will not have a page for you until your book is actually published. Prior to publication, you may want to connect with your audience. The pre-publication connection builds demand for your book and can help you make sure that your book will meet the needs of your intended audience. The "name the book" contest we discussed in the last chapter is an example of how a pre-publication web presence can help you prepare for the success of your book.

Take stock of your current online resources by making a list of anything you already have in place online. Do you have a website, a Facebook page, a Google group, a Pinterest account, a Twitter feed, etc.? After you have your list developed, make a list of all the other online resources where you know someone who is successful. For instance, you might be on LinkedIn, but your friend is a big user of Facebook.

Review the internet presence that you already have. Is your online image consistent with how you want to be known/found when your book is published? If not, now is the time to do some clean-up. If so, where can you begin to announce that you are writing and/or publishing a book? What internet resources do you think you will need? Do you believe you will need your own website? Will a Facebook fan page be enough? Many authors develop their own websites. This gives them some flexibility for their message, and it allows them to directly sell services, products and digital media. Earlier I mentioned that some authors pre-sell books. In order to do something like this, you will need to have a website. Other services like Facebook may have rules against selling items from your page. Always make sure you are following the rules to assure that you will not have problems as you build your connection to your audience.

Website development can quickly become very expensive. Do your best to be budget conscious on website building in the early stages of your business. Do your homework. Start simple and be careful of buying more than you need to start. Remember that you will be able to develop resources like this when you begin to have an income from your book. Do your research, stay within your budget and develop a professional and functional site that meets your needs. Many service providers offer "packages" of website services. Some of these can get very expensive very quickly. Be aware of who will have control and ownership of the content. Some site developers will be difficult to separate from if they control your content and you decide to move on to a different way of doing your website.

I have a slightly more complete discussion of website costs and issues in my *Jump-Start Guide for a Start-Up Online Business*. If you are interested, contact me through my website, and I will let you know how to get a free copy of the eBook.

Building a website and using the social networking capacity of the internet will take time. Make a commitment to work on building your online presence on a regular basis. When you are launching your book, try to get exposure on as many platforms as possible by asking your friends and people who may be interested to make an announcement on whatever platform they use. You don't have to have an account/profile on every system, but it will help if you know people on most of the major social networking sites.

Why Publish Independently?

I asked you to consider at least four possible models for getting your book published. After carefully researching the options, you will need to select the best model for you and for your book. Remember to read the fine print, try to know as much as possible about the model you choose and consider hiring an attorney to facilitate your review of the contracts and legal implications of the model you choose. Who will ultimately hold the copyright and rights to publication is an important consideration. Each model has possible advantages for an author. In my experience, authors are most confused by and need more information about the independent publishing processes.

In this chapter, I want to encourage you to look at the independent publishing tools that are available for eBooks and Print on Demand (POD). The independent publishing process can be a good way to learn. It can also be the model that gives you the most control over costs. That said, it can also be very expensive if you do not exercise your best planning and judgment. Because you are inexperienced, someone may easily sell you something you may not need. They will make it sound very good. They will try to convince you that you NEED whatever they are selling. It might sound like it is essential that you buy a lot of services, products, etc. If you are prone to saying "YES" to great sounding offers, independent publishing could be a tricky process for you. Do your research and compare possible purchases to assure the best option at the best price for the best value.

Staying in your budget is an important goal. When you plan your budget, if you are easily sold things that you cannot afford, you may benefit from gathering a group of like-minded writers to help each other stay on track and within budget. You may also consider interviewing some book coaches and finding someone who is good at independent publishing with an eye toward cost containment. You may spend less in the long run by having a trusted and experienced coach who can help you make good choices that will assure your likely profitability. Remember, however, the choice of hiring a coach will also add to your budget.

Independent publishing also affords you a remarkable influence over the time frame for your publication. An eBook can be available for sale online within a few hours or a day or two from when you upload your files. This helps when you are planning announcements, events and wanting to create meaningful partnerships for mutual promotion. The process for publishing a POD paperback is also cost effective and reasonably quick in turnaround. The print copy will take a little more time to set up, and you will want to review proofs before you finalize the book for sale. Depending on your level of expertise and the level of skill for anyone you may hire for assistance, you may need to order your proof several times. The POD provider will need time to print the book and ship it. You will have costs associated with each proof and the related shipping. Remember if you have to make changes after you publish a paperback, you will also need to pay for making the changes.

Using Amazon

If you are willing to publish independently, select the platform/ format that you personally have the most experience using. I have done most of my learning on the Amazon systems. I have published the Kindle version eBooks using Kindle Direct Publishing (KDP). This is not an endorsement for the Amazon platform; however, it is a popular choice and will inform my examples.

In order to publish your eBook you will need: 1. The completed manuscript properly formatted with a hyperlinked Table of Contents (TOC) 2. The exact title of your book 3. An eBook cover file (1:6 ratio, RGB colors, minimum 625 X 1000 pixels; maximum 1563 X 2500 pixels) 4. A brief description of your book 5. A list of key words related to your title and topic and 6. A short biography of yourself.

I publish the eBook version of my work on the Kindle Direct Publishing (KDP) platform first. Set up your KDP account through the KDP website. The KDP account will use your Amazon account information (username is the email address and the password you established). I order the book cover design about a month before I will be ready to publish the book. You may order the eBook covers affordably on micro job sites. I am generally able to obtain quality book covers and the original source files for around $50. You usually pay extra for the source file. The source file is the graphic file in the program the artist used to design the cover (Adobe Illustrator or Photoshop are common). Always pay to get the source files. Later you will need them for the paperback cover design. You may also need them if you ever make any changes or upgrades to the cover. I often ask the designer to also create one marketing piece with the cover (bookmark, postcard, flyer or business card). The marketing piece features the book cover and any other message that I want to use to promote the book. If you know everything that will be on the paperback cover, consider having the artist design the paperback cover at the same time or in close succession. The difficulty with this is related to the adjustments that have to be made on the cover of the paperback. The paperback cover requires a page count so that you can calculate the spine width. You may also find that the cover has to be adjusted for the colors that print. These are the most common paperback cover adjustments among my clients.

As you can see, the costs associated with the eBook will be very affordable. The cost of the cover, some marketing and the purchase of the ISBN with my publishing company are less than $75. Even if the book sells for a modest price, I should be able to break even with the sale of an attainable number of books. Once I break even, I may be able to fund the publication of the paperback through the proceeds of the eBook.

The Amazon KDP website has tutorials and helpful information about formatting your book, uploading your files and describing the entire process. Make time to read through the instructions and watch the tutorials. Once you upload your files, you will get a message from KDP that they are processing/reviewing the file and that it can take up to a few days. When they have finished reviewing the file, they will send you a file with markings for you to review. This might involve formatting errors. Review each one carefully. Return to your file that you uploaded and make any appropriate changes. Then upload the file again to repeat the process. Once you have a file without any marked errors that need to be addressed, you will be able to publish the book. Your eBook will be available on Amazon very quickly.

Once your book is available on Amazon, go to Author Central on Amazon: https://authorcentral.amazon.com/. Develop your profile on Amazon with a brief biography, a link to your blog, a listing of any events related to your book and a book trailer if you have one.

If you are only publishing an eBook, you are in business. Find ways to connect with your readers and set up a schedule for marketing and having KDP promotions to make your eBook available for free download. According to the research I read, for about every 100 free copies downloaded, there will be one sale. You will want to make sure you get plenty of exposure on the internet to assure that your KDP promotions are successful.

If you are also publishing a paperback edition of your book, use your KDP promotion to contact people that you would like to have read your book and give you a quote/testimonial that you may be able to use in your marketing or on the cover of your paperback. You may want 5 – 10 testimonials that you could use to attract prospective readers. Asking prospective respondents/reviewers to obtain the free eBook on the KDP promotion day is an easy way to get the book to the respondent. You might also want to include a little instruction sheet explaining how to get the free copy, how to get a free Kindle Reader App for a computer, tablet or phone and what kind of information you need for using a quote from a respondent. I will send you a sample of a form I used if you contact me through my website.

Create Space

Amazon publishes paperbacks on demand through Create Space. You will set up a Create Space account with your Amazon information just as you did for KDP. Again, there are tutorials and information about independent publishing through Create Space that are worth your time.

The process of producing a paperback is a little more involved and a little more expensive than the eBook. In addition to having the well-written, well-edited and meticulously proofread manuscript, you will also need some artistic/design elements. The book cover that you used on KDP was just the front of the book. The paperback will have the front, spine and back. Take a minute and look at a paperback book. The back of the book will be the side of the page to the left, followed by the spine and then by the front. In some ways this appears counter intuitive. You will need a little time to get the cover before you are ready to publish your book. Make sure you give yourself and your artist enough time for the cover design. Unless you have some experience (and perhaps a program like InDesign by Adobe) with the interior layout and design of the pages, you may need to hire a book designer. Book designers can cost from a few hundred to several thousand dollars. The length of your book will be a factor. How many charts, graphs, photos or other artistic elements you have in your book will influence the costs. The number of pages in your book will influence how wide the spine of the book cover will be. This may require some adjustment after you see the first proof. The designer will often charge by the hour and may have charges for corrections after the initial layout is complete. Try to find a designer that will work with you for a flat fee. Then, be very conscientious about having everything proofed and clean before you start. Making changes that you have to pay for later is often budget-breaking. The interior design artist will also be able to do the cover layout. You will get two files from the designer to upload on Create Space. The cover file will be one file with the back, spine and front just as it will print for the book cover. The covers are usually done in full color. The interior file will be everything that prints on the pages of the book. An experienced designer will plan the pages to be visually attractive and correctly spaced for the binding. When you upload the files, you will need to know if the pages have "bleed" to the edges. Usually the cover does and the interior pages do not. Ask your designer about this before you upload the files. "Bleed" refers to the use of margins. If the color bleeds all the way off the edge or a picture bleeds across two pages, the answer is "yes." The designer will also leave a white box on the back of the cover. Create Space will put the ISBN Barcode in this box. You do not need to pay for a barcode from Bowker. The Create Space barcode will not encode the price. Create Space will also need the last page of the book to be blank for a bar code and printing information that they need to insert in every book. This is the last page that faces the inside cover.

Ask your designer to waive additional charges if you want to add a few quotes/testimonials to the back of your book cover after the proofs are available. If that is not possible, try to create a printed version to distribute (use a watermark indicating it is a review copy). You may also want to publish the eBook first and have the KDP promotion for a free download for your prospective reviewers. If you need the quotes first for the designer, make sure you get them before you order the cover to control costs.

When designing your book, think about your audience. You will also want to think about how people will acquire your book. You will want to think of how they may carry the book around. Some paperbacks that people carry around are convenient when the book is small. The size of the book is called the trim size. When you select a trim size, you may need to take portability and shipping into consideration. I frequently mail copies of my books. When I was deciding on a trim size, I selected a size for the book (5.06 inches X 7.81 inches) that would easily fit into a size zero padded envelope that I regularly have on hand for mailing. Review the available trim sizes on Create Space before you start interviewing designers. Think about anything that might be important to consider and discuss it with the designer. If you will be selling books at events, you may also want to consider making the books easy to carry and ship. The trim size of the book is an aesthetic process but also a practical consideration. Beginning with the end in mind could save you money down the road.

Amazon offers some paid services through Create Space. They offer some free templates for the do-it-yourselfer, and they have a range of paid services if you need help. They offer paid services for design, editing and marketing. The prices are posted online for the standard services. The prices appear to be affordable. I have reviewed copies of books that have used the paid services, and I would rate the outcome as adequate/average. You will want to do your own comparison shopping for the services you need to purchase. The advantage on Create Space is that there is a feel of one-stop shopping, reasonable pricing and a nice range of service packages. You may compare their services to providers on micro job sites or other author services that you will be able to find online. Remember that Create Space also offers a package for converting your paperback to the Kindle version (doing the formatting) if you are publishing the paperback first or publishing the Kindle version and the paperback to come out at the same time. At this time, I have not used any of the Amazon paid services.

Get it Written

Learning how to publish a book is what takes your writing out to the audience in the best vehicle you can afford. It is to your advantage if you know something about how you will publish your book before it is completed. You will be able to plan and develop the publishing schedule as a part of the book-writing process.

The first book is usually the hardest. In this case, try to have the first draft fully completed before you start to plan the publishing. This allows you to learn the publishing steps without taking energy away from your writing. In time, you will want to be able to overlap the writing process and the publishing process to improve the speed of publication. I often have clients who are still in the writing process. Everyone has a writing process. Pay attention and learn to become better at the writing process that works for you. This will also give you the ability to know when to begin working on the publishing process. For example, I am very good at planning my writing and knowing about how long each section takes me to write. I can easily determine when the writing will be finished. If you have a completed draft, you will want to start working on the publication process as you begin revising.

After you have a completed first draft, reread, revise and make sure you run spell check and grammar check. When you have a clean first draft that is about as good as you can make it, take it to a writing group or find another way to get feedback and input. People who are similar to your target audience would be a very good type of first readers. Find out what questions they have and what they think would make the book better (i.e., more interesting). Make more revisions based on the feedback. This second draft may be the place to consider hiring an editor. You are not asking for the editor to proofread! Some of that is likely in the editorial process, but the more important contribution of the editor will be to help you improve your writing. The editor will help make suggestions for consistency, readability, clarity and overall organization.

This is the place where your budget skills are on the line. Professional editing is an important contribution to the quality of your book. The chief complaint that readers have about independently published books involves the quality of the book. The solution to this problem is using a good editor. Interview prospective editors. Have a clear description of your manuscript, the number of pages, the number of words and a little about your writing experience. Ask for a sample edit and a price quote up front. You may get an idea of costs from http://www.the-efa.org/res/rates.php. Stay within your budget and create a good working relationship with your editor.

While the editor is working on the editing process, you will be able to create the additional copy that you will need for your book. By now you should have a title and a brief book description. You may want to write the book description in a longer and shorter form. You may want to have a descriptive line/sentence about your book. Think of this as a tagline to catch the attention of the prospective reader. You will also need a short paragraph about yourself. This "about the author" biography paragraph may go on the book cover/jacket and may also be used on the Author Central page or on your website. Also, make sure you have any other copy you will need for your book. You will need a title page, a copyright page, and you may want to have other information at the front or the back of your book. Some authors include a dedication, acknowledgements or a foreword (written by someone other than the author). If you have a number of figures, illustrations or tables, you may want to have a list of those at the back of the book. You may also consider writing a preface or an introduction to your book. If you are learning about the parts of the book by doing internet research, these elements are referred to as the "front matter" of a book. In the eBook, more of this type of information may appear at the end. The reason for this is that only a certain percentage of your book will show in the Amazon "Look Inside" feature. Typically, the look inside sample will offer about the first 10% of the book. A prospective reader/buyer may want to see the actual content of your book when they look inside. By assuring that the text of the book is not delayed for more than 5% or so of the total number of pages, you have a better chance that the potential reader will get a taste of your book and get to the first chapter. Keep this strategy in mind when you are writing the material that will be at the front of your book. You want to have writing that will grab the attention of readers, getting them to want to keep reading and buy the book.

Proofreading

After you receive the edited manuscript and make the changes that will improve your book, you are ready to proofread in earnest. You may need an editor again if you are not good at proofreading. You may also benefit from the help of some trusted friends who are good at proofreading. In my experience, if you are using multiple proofreaders, you are probably better off using hard/printed copies for each reader. If everyone proofreading is a very proficient computer user, you may be able to use the "track changes" feature in the Microsoft Word program. If you use that, remember that you will need to pull a copy of the finished document over onto the notepad to strip out the code snippets that will be abundant in a file where you have used track changes.

When you have a clean, well-edited, carefully proofed document, you are ready to start formatting your eBook or designing your paperback for publication.

Formatting and Design

An eBook is formatted; a paperback is designed. Remember to copy the entire book into notepad. Then copy the notepad file and bring it into a clean New Document in your word processor. This is a first step in formatting your eBook to avoid some of the most difficult formatting issues.

In your New Document, you will begin adding in only the essential formatting. When formatting your eBook, remember to set up your TOC with the hyperlinks to help the reader navigate your book. Use a 12 point type for the text. The chapter titles will be larger because you used the styles for "Heading." If you are publishing an eBook, refer to the chapter with formatting tips in this book for assistance. I have included general instructions for creating the TOC in the appendix.

If you are publishing a paperback or print version of your book, consider using a template for your interior files or using a program specifically created for doing this type of book layout. The most common software for this is InDesign by Adobe. The program is more sophisticated than a novice can comfortably navigate. I have been successful using it when I paid a designer with experience to set up the "Master Pages" so that I had a template to use. Having my own Master Page template set up let me have some input on the layout that I did not have on the templates that were available through Create Space/Amazon. Once you have the template or Master Page file, paste your clean (codeless) manuscript in the template. This page layout will have page numbers and a Table of Contents with page numbers. Keep careful watch of the page numbers. As you move or change things in the file, you may need to update the page numbers. The most common formatting error I have experienced is the text on the page getting too close to the page number, the page number/s not printing, the page numbering in the Table of Contents being inaccurate, and the text of a page running too close to the margin or falling into the binding. This is corrected by being a little more generous with your margins. A book designer may need to help you calculate the best margins, particularly regarding the margin that will be closest to the binding on the page. The calculation can be influenced by how may pages you have in your book. The book designer will also help you with the placement of charts, graphs, graphics or pictures. You will need to know if the book will require "bleed" when you upload the file. If you have any pictures or graphics that go across two pages, you will have bleed. If that is something you are doing in your book, you should probably use a designer for the book. If you are trying to use templates, make sure you have placed the pictures on pages that will be facing each other.

In the print version, you will also get to select a font. A designer can help steer you toward a good font for your type of book. You may also want to read the articles on Create Space/ Amazon about preparing your book for print. There are many clean fonts that will help your book appear professional and easy on the eyes of your reader.

The print version of the book will require two files for uploading on Create Space. You will have the cover file. It contains the back, spine and front. The designer should save this file as a PDF. You will very likely have bleed to the edges on the cover. The interior file should also be converted into a PDF with every page of the book included. This file includes the Title Page, Copyright Page, any other front matter, the Table of Contents and the text of your book. At the back of the book, you may have any other material that the reader may need. This might include resources for further information, an order form to obtain additional copies in bulk from you, contact information or anything else you want to communicate to the reader.

Once you upload the files, Create Space will review the files and send them back to you with possible errors marked. You will go through this review process before you are able to order a proof copy of your printed book. Use the review process to clean up as many errors as possible. I usually order at least two proof copies if I have used a designer. I send one copy to the designer, and I keep one copy to review for further proofreading. When I get the proof, I will look at the layout and the cover. I want to notice any problems and make sure that everything looks professional and ready for the reader. I usually have a number of changes at this point. Look carefully at everything. The cover of one book we published came out a different color than we thought it would. The dark blue of the cover background swallowed the dark color type of the title. We made modifications to assure that the title was visible and that the cover was clean and professional looking. The spine also requires some adjustment. You want to make sure the information on the spine is properly centered and professional looking. Put your book on your bookshelf next to other paperbacks and see how it looks by comparison. This is a glance test for judging your book by its cover. Remember that I mailed a proof copy to the designer. The designer gets the extra proof copy I sent within a few days. That gives me a head start for checking everything. The designer may notice things that require adjustment/change. When I am making edits and changes, I can ask the designer by phone to look at the same proof copy. Once you make all of the changes that are necessary for the first proof, the designer will send you the corrected files. You will upload these to Create Space/Amazon. I always order a proof after the first round of changes based on the proof. If there wasn't really anything that had to be adjusted artistically in the cover or the page layouts, I may only order one copy of the proof this time. When I get the second proof, I make sure all of my edits from the first proof are corrected. I also read through the proof again to make sure there are not any other changes/corrections or errors. If I need to make more changes, I may order yet another proof after I make the changes. You may repeat this process as often as necessary.

Every proof copy costs money to print and ship. It may take a few weeks for the book to be printed and shipped to you. Plan the costs of proofs in your budget. When you order the likely "last" proof copy, you should be able to plan when your book will be available for sale. You will begin marketing the publication date as soon as you can predict when your book will be available. Plan this with more time than the publication might take. You will have more opportunity to get the message out. For example, if you think your book will be available for sale in 2 – 3 weeks from when you upload the last corrected files, you might want to indicate it will be available in 4-6 weeks. I have had quick turn around on most of my books. However, I had one that was being published in November/December, and it was delayed for printing because of the holidays. If you are planning a book to sell during the holidays, publish it in September/October.

If the last proof is clean with very few changes needed and you want to obtain some reviews/testimonials for your marketing, you should order multiple copies of the last proof. These copies will say PROOF in the cover, but they will allow you to circulate some copies and obtain the testimonials. Then the designer can add them to the book or cover before you complete and publish the book.

Once you have approved the proof and the book moves into the publication phase at Create Space/Amazon, you will have to pay if you have any need to make further changes. This is another place for budget consciousness. Make sure your proof is ready before you move to publication. I know one author who forgot to carefully check the proofs. She missed some pages of her manuscript that were never copied into the layout template. Since she had already published the book, she had to pay to make the corrections.

Preview Reviews

Obtain some reviews from people who are likely to benefit from your book. If you can think of people who are important in your field, you may want to send them a free copy of your book and ask them to make a short comment to encourage others to read your book. You will want to give a clear deadline and then follow up a week before your deadline. You may have a form for the reader to complete. The form should include a space for the reviewers to make the comment and a statement that they sign giving you permission to use the comment and their identifying information on the book cover and any marketing material.

If you are paying to make changes to your paperback file, you might print the cover without the testimonials and then just re-do the cover. If you find that you also need to reupload the interior files, you may want to include in the back of the book any of the additional testimonials that you receive. You might have an extra page or two at the end of your book. Testimonials can be a good use for the space.

Marketing

This chapter is a mini lesson in marketing your book. Your great book only becomes great when your audience finds it. Your job is to make sure your potential audience finds out about your book. Reading the blog, articles and books related to marketing will help you learn how to develop the best marketing plan for your book.

Step one – look at your budget. How are you doing? Were you able to contain costs, or did you already spend more than you planned? Take stock of your resources now. I hope that you are under budget at this point or right on the plan. You probably included some money for marketing. How much?

Develop a habit of noticing what you can easily and quickly do that costs little or no money and lets people know about your book.

Identify the likely date that you are confident that your book will be available. Your "launch" date should be about 4 – 6 weeks away. Now that you have an approximate date, look at some calendars online that include holidays and special events. Look at dates near when your book will be available. Are there any already identified "celebrations" that would make an interesting combination with your book title, category or intended audience. This can help you market your book.

You may also be able to identify organizations that share your interest in your book topic. Consider contacting organizations that have a common interest. See if they would be interested in partnering with you for an event or inviting you to come and speak.

Identify any independent bookstores in your area or other local venues that would make a nice match for your topic. Based on this preliminary research, identify a likely date, place and time to coordinate a book event to announce and launch your new book. Contact the venue and make the arrangements for your book event. Be creative, make it fun and plan the event as thoroughly as possible. Invite friends and colleagues to be sure you have an audience.

Once you have the book launch information, develop a press release (sometimes identified more broadly as a media release). Make sure the press release is interesting, timely and includes all of the essential information (who, what, when, where, why). Remember to proofread carefully. You can find examples online. You may also use the micro job sites if you have money in your budget for obtaining professional help writing the press release. Once you have a good press release, begin sending it (or variations of it) once a week to a free online press release submission service. Try several different ones so that you get a good idea of how they work. Keep track of which services you use. You will want to see which service and which week works best for getting the word out.

As you get closer to the launch event, you will want to find more ways to share the news locally and distribute your marketing material. Send postcards; distribute bookmarks or business cards with your book cover on them. Print a label with information about your launch event and put the label on the back of the marketing material. You may want to create a free Quick Response (QR) code online and include it on the marketing material. The QR code should take the scanner to the URL for your website sales page. People can scan the QR code, and it will open the web browser on their phone to your website page where you can have the details about the event and information about purchasing the book. I often create 8½" x 11" flyers and post them around the community with the QR code. I can track the information on how many times the QR code is scanned. You will not have a sales page on Amazon until your book is available. If you do not have a website, consider starting a blog. You will need an online destination for the QR code to offer a point of sale.

Contact your local media and provide them with your

press/media release for your event and your book. If you can manage to get an interview on radio or television, you may be able to link to the archived media from your website. This type of opportunity boosts your visibility, and it also improves your credibility.

Promote pre-registration for your book event. A number of free services online allow you to schedule an event and have people register for the event. Have the venue post the registration information on its website. Search for free event registration services. If you are using venues that frequently host book events, they will probably have ways that they promote the events.

Plan your book event carefully. Practice and polish what you will do during the event to make the connection with your audience. Make the event fun for everyone who comes. Have someone introduce you, prepare a few remarks or a short talk about how you wrote your book, read an interesting passage from your book and invite questions from the audience. If you are at a venue that does not sell books, be sure to order books from Create Space and bring them to the event. Have a friend come and sell the books at the event. Offer a discount for purchase at the event. You may want to have all of the attendees fill out their names and email addresses on a ticket or paper to enter a drawing for a free copy of the book. This can be a great way to start building your mailing list of fans. Think about how you would like to sign the books and select a good pen for using during the signing. Your tag line or a special salutation may make your autographed copy more meaningful.

There could be several advantages for you to order some books at your cost from Create Space. If you are having your event at an independent bookseller or a venue that usually has a bookseller that makes the sales, offer to provide the books. Sell them to the bookseller at the distributor's rate (usually 50% off the cover price). Offer to bring and sell them the exact number that sells at the event PLUS any additional copies wanted for the store.

In order to encourage people who come to the event to buy a book, you may want to offer a discount. You may not be able to offer a discount to the audience if you are working with the bookseller. This will depend on the cover price of your book and your cost to purchase the books. You may want to ask the bookseller to split any "event" price discount. For example, if your book cover price is $14.00 and a reseller is handling the sales, you would be selling the books to the reseller for $7.00. If the reseller agrees, you may offer to sell the books for $13 at the event. However, you would split the dollar discount with the reseller. Discuss this with the reseller before the event. If the reseller does not agree, you would need to absorb the entire dollar amount or agree that the books would be sold at the cover price. If this happens, see if you can offer something in addition to your book if participants make the purchase at the event. Order the books from Create Space/Amazon and then prepare an invoice/receipt for the number of books sold. Ask the bookseller to bring a check or credit card to pay you that evening. You will need a card reader or method to receive any credit card payments. You should get paid at the end of the event. The bookseller will have the exact quantity and will not need to make returns of surplus (the extra copies cannot be returned). The advantage is that you will make your portion at the event. Otherwise, it takes some time before you are paid royalties on the wholesale discounted sales through Create Space.

Selling books directly will often involve collecting and remitting sales tax. Check with your accountant regarding the requirements for this in your state and the local tax jurisdiction. If the bookseller at your event is collecting and remitting sales tax, you will not need to do that on the sale of the same book. Obtain the most accurate information from your local tax professional.

As soon as you get all of the details settled for your book launch event, begin to plan the next year. Do something every month (every week if you can commit the time and money) to promote your book. Schedule a specific activity every four weeks. This may include additional live events where you plan and promote being in places with your readers. Expand your online presence. Create a fan page on Facebook; develop a presence on additional social networking sites. Create a regular schedule for blogging and sending tweets on Twitter. Update your website periodically. Develop a book trailer if you don't have one yet. Post it on YouTube, the Author Central page on Amazon and on your website.

When you look at your twelve-month marketing plan, make sure you also create a budget that is realistic and that you are confident that you can commit to spending. You may hire help with some activities. Include the financial resources for any paid services. For example, you may want to run a print ad in a publication or you may want to run a Google adwords campaign.

Free Download Promotion

Using the marketing plan you outlined, look for opportunities where a free download of your eBook would be a great visibility booster. The KDP system gives you 5 days every 90 days that you will be able to use for giving away your eBook. The instructions for setting up a campaign for the free download are available on the KDP website. Plan the downloads with at least 3 – 4 weeks lead time. When you are having a promotional free download, be sure to put up flyers with the QR code indicating that people can get the free download by scanning your QR code.

Any time you have a free download promotion, post the information on your website. Send out a press release. On the day of the download, try to have people you know on every social networking platform communicate that the book is available for free download.

If you have an event where you are not able to sell books for some reason, offer to set up a free download the day of your event or the day after. If you do it the same day, you can pass a flyer around with the QR code on it. The audience members can just scan the code while they are there at the event. Make some flyers available for people who want to obtain the book at home. This can be a great rapport builder when you have the opportunity to speak to a group but not offer anything for sale.

Informational Products

Develop some valuable companion products that complement the content of your book. You might have a guide for book groups, a tip sheet or a custom list that would help your audience achieve something in your book. You may also want to record some presentations or some reading excerpts from your book. You can post the bonus information on your website or in a client only section that you reserve for audience members who register with your site. Some handouts may be the add-ons for the on-site book purchase when you cannot offer a discount.

Develop these companion products around the questions that readers ask you or the needs that they express. I developed an Excel spreadsheet for readers of my *Jump-Start Guide for a Start-Up Online Business*. You may also develop power point presentations, webinars and teleclasses that you can record and make available again and again. I plan to offer an annual teleclass for writers who are publishing a first book. The teleclass this year was helpful for the participants and helped me understand their questions and the places where they had difficulty. It made this book a more useful guide. Using what I learn from the participants, I will provide resource lists and information on my website to help readers.

Give Aways

Any time that I speak to a group, I give a handout that has information for the audience. I also include information about my books, my website and other relevant resources. In addition to the KDP promotions where you give the eBook away for free, look for other ways to offer your book without charge. If I speak to a group where I cannot sell books, I charge enough for speaking to give copies of a book.

I often give free paperback copies of the *Jump-Start Guide for a Start-Up Online Business* to my counseling and coaching clients. It informs some of our conversations and is a good reminder to them of the work that we are doing. The book is a tool that I developed around some specific types of conversations that I often have with my clients.

I also give a certain number of books from one of the titles that I published to selected not-for-profit groups. These donations help potential readers find out about the book. It helps the group raise funds for good work. The more people who know about the book, the more potential buyers I will reach. This also energizes my relationship with the not-for-profit group.

Develop some partnerships or affiliate relationships. Offer your book or some of your information products to the customers of someone (an affiliate) who is effective at reaching your target audience. Usually the affiliate agrees to send an email or host an event with you. The affiliate offers the opportunity to sign up for your product (or event) through your website to the members on the affiliate's email list. The affiliate agrees to do this for a percentage of the sales you make, or for something from which the affiliate benefits. Affiliate relationships help you develop an email list. Affiliates are people you might notify before book events. Invite the affiliate to come and meet you at an event. When you develop relationships with affiliates you will let affiliates know about your upcoming books and other creative endeavors.

Offer to participate in calls/interviews or other information sharing with affiliates that will interest your target audience. If there are products sold as a result of your participation, you may share sales revenue. Volunteer to write articles or guest blog postings for sites with a good following of your target audience. The most successful affiliate relationships are mutually beneficial, and more importantly, are valuable partnerships in the view of the target audience.

Book Events

Creating events that engage your audience can be an effective strategy to attract readers. Look for trade shows, organizations that have a common interest, holiday events and local retailers. Launch events at the beginning of the life of your book are just a beginning. Offer to hold events anywhere your target audience is likely to find you. Consider having an event calendar on your website to help people find you and have the opportunity to meet you at an event.

In addition to events where you appear in person, you may want to create some online events. Consider hosting a teleseminar, a conference call, a webinar or see if someone who regularly holds cyber events would allow you to appear on their event as a guest. You may be able to record events and offer them on your website. This gives you an opportunity to connect to your audience in meaningful ways, and you can simultaneously develop content for your website.

Business Processes

At the beginning of this book, I wrote about the business of writing and publishing. As I conclude the book, I want to encourage you to view your writing as part of an entrepreneurial endeavor. Learning some basic business processes and how to consistently follow the plan you develop will help you experience more success as an author. The most successful authors (even the ones who publish independently) are always improving and working on their next book. Developing effective business processes may involve researching and deciding on what kind of a business you will operate for publishing your books. You may want to be a sole proprietor or you may want to form a corporation. Discuss the options with your attorney or tax professional before establishing your publishing company.

Use a basic bookkeeping system. You will have tax implications from your income. You may need to pay self-employment taxes on a quarterly basis. Plan some of your expenses at a time of the year that will offer you some tax advantages. Good tax planning and advice from your tax professional could help you navigate the best time to incur expenses and offset income. You may also be required to collect and remit sales tax. Many publishers, who sell their own books, use a merchant account or a credit card reader that attaches to a smart phone and can put money in the bank as soon as they scan the credit card. Many of these programs will calculate the sales tax rate and add it to the sale at the time of the purchase.

The more often you publish a book, the more efficient you will become with the process. Keep notes about what you had to do and things that you want to remember for next time. Create a writing schedule and start planning your next book. You may also want to co-author a book with someone with more experience as a writer and/or a publisher. Identify someone who has different skills from yours. Work together and learn from each other. Find a peer to learn some technical skills together or to learn some marketing tasks from each other. Barter with each other for the tasks that use each person's strengths. Go back to the skills assessment that you did earlier. Look for the greatest strengths you might be able to use to help someone else.

You may also use your strengths to actually provide services on the micro job sites. Write book reviews, press releases or copy for websites/marketing. This may be a place to start if you need to raise funds to meet your budget for your book publishing. You may also try to use some of the crowd funding resources (e.g., kickstarter) to raise funds and pre-sell books. Having an accurate budget will be very important. You will want to be sure that the funding would be adequate to publish the book.

Use your skills, tell your story, get your message to the market and may all your goals be exceeded.

Tips

Kindle Direct Publishing (KDP) First eBook Tips

Preparing the file for an eBook:

- Create a clean file for the interior of your eBook

- Complete all of your writing in a word processing program

- Highlight (Select) all of the text and copy it (CTRL+C)

- Copy to the NOTEPAD (on a PC this is a program they all have)
- Paste onto the notepad (CTRL+V)

- Use the notepad because it will "strip" all of the special codes out of the file

- Highlight on the Notepad, HIGHLIGHT everything copy it (CTRL+C)

- Open a new document in your Word Processor and paste the file (CTRL+V)

- Develop the Table of Contents (TOC) and insert pictures, etc.

- USE Formatting sparingly if at all (i.e., no indents, bold, line spacing changes, etc.)

- Convert the file when it is clean and to your satisfaction, convert it to a PDF (HTML if you know HTML)

- Upload this interior file to Amazon KDP

- Review the file - Amazon KDP will let you "look through" the book in a "viewer"

- Look at each marked error; the KDP viewer will mark possible problems

- Try to clean up and fix anything here by going back to your original document (and repeat the whole process); and/or you may go back to the version you had after you pasted it from notepad

- Upload the file after you make revisions and clean the file

- Review the file again after you upload it

- Repeat this process as often as needed

- Send it for publication once you feel like you have most things the way you want them

- Wait for the KDP file review – Amazon KDP will review it (usually takes a few days) and then the book will be available on Amazon

The KDP Process

Go to
https://kdp.amazon.com/

It will come back as:
https://kdp.amazon.com/self-publishing/signin

Sign in with your Amazon Account or set up an account if you need one.

Watch this tutorial video and follow the instructions (some of the screens look a little different, because the video is older, but it is a great overview of the process.)

http://www.youtube.com/watch?v=kVtOL9uth40 (This is an easy overview… about 5.5 minutes.)

https://kdp.amazon.com/self-publishing/
help?topicId=A2M7MM0UP7PHK0 (This Amazon created version is a little longer, but it is more thorough.)

Key points and recommended choices

- Do not list Amazon as the Publisher

- DO NOT fill in the ISBN number field for an eBook (unless you purchased one from Bowker for the eBook format specifically)

- Indicate that you have the publishing rights for your work and for your cover

- Select a BISAC category for your book

- Add Key words (We can improve this later)

- Upload the Product Image (it is your jpg file for the cover)

- Choose how you want to manage the rights - Digital Rights Management (It is usually okay to select "DO NOT enable...") Do some research if you have questions or qualms about this – This cannot be changed once you make a choice

- Upload your "book" content file [usually a pdf with a working (hyperlinked) table of contents]

- Select worldwide rights

- Select the Royalty option 70%

- Type in the price of your book that you want your reader to pay

- Check the box for Amazon to calculate the international rates

- Allow "Lending" (again research this if you are not sure you would want Amazon Prime members to be able to borrow your book)

- Click on the terms and save and publish

- Remember that Amazon has to review the files. They will tell you if there are problems, and you will have the opportunity to fix them. Sometimes it is okay to publish regardless.

Other Hints

- Select a small project first
- Learn on a short document - when learning to format, it helps if you have a relatively short document
- SCAN any tables or charts and then INSERT the scanned image in a .JPG file format
- CENTER the image on the page
- Consider breaking a large project into a few small "teaser" projects so you will be able to learn as you go

If you have a budget for some assistance, try contractors at micro job websites like Fiverr.com, Fourerr.com or oDesk. The oDesk contractors will be more expensive, but they may be available for future projects. If using contractors – make sure they send you the "source" files at the end (InDesign, Photoshop, Adobe Illustrator are the most common formats). There is sometimes an extra charge for the source files. My experience indicates it is best to maintain the source files on your own computer.

Creating an Active (Hyperlinked) Table of Contents

Table of Contents Method for eBooks

As I mentioned, I am not an expert at this. I have a rough summary of this method here.

I suggest that you review it, try it, do some additional research for easier ways or decide if this is something you will need to hire help to do. If you know you are hiring help for this, just skip this section of the book.

Select everything in your manuscript (press Ctrl and A keys at the same time).

In the Home ribbon, set the Font size to 12.

While all of the text is still highlighted, in the Styles ribbon, press the Normal button.

Highlight the Title of the book on the Title page. Apply the Heading 1 style.

Then go through your book highlighting each chapter title. When a chapter title is highlighted, apply the Heading 2 style and then press Align Text Left. Make sure you do this for every chapter.

You will also want to use the Insert ribbon and press the Page Break button at the beginning of every chapter.

Return to the beginning of your document.

After the Title page, use the Insert ribbon and press the Page Break.

After the copyright page, use the Insert ribbon and press the Page Break.

On the next (blank page), enter the TITLE, Table of Contents and press ENTER.

Move the cursor to the beginning of the name of your first chapter.

Press the ENTER key. Move the cursor to the blank line you created. Press the space bar a few times and select (highlight) the whole empty line you just created.

Press "First Normal" in the Home ribbon. Do this for every chapter.

Go back to the first chapter heading and place the cursor at the beginning of the empty line. On the Insert ribbon, press bookmark. Give the bookmark a name similar to the chapter title. (Do not use special characters, punctuation, symbols or spaces.) You may use numbers, but the bookmark name has to start with a letter.

Click Add (You won't see the bookmark).

Create a similar bookmark for each chapter in your book.

Return to the Table of Contents page that you made.

After the words Table of Contents, press ENTER.

Select the VIEW on the ribbon at the top.

Press SPLIT.

Place the separator in the middle of the program window.

Scroll down to the words Table of Contents (in the upper window).

In the lower window, scroll down to the next heading (chapter title).

Copy and paste the heading from your text (lower window) to your Table of Contents (upper window of Word).

Do this for every chapter heading.

When you are finished, place the cursor in the lower window and in the VIEW ribbon press the Remove SPLIT button.

In the HOME button on the ribbon, press the Show/Hide button and delete extra spaces at the end of each line in your Table of Contents if there are any. Then unpress the Show/Hide button.

Apply the Heading 2 style to the title and the First Normal style to the text of your Table of Contents.

Select the whole table of contents (the heading and the chapter titles) and press the Align Text Left button.

Increase spacing between items in your TOC by adding a line at the end of each chapter name (SHIFT and ENTER key at the same time).

Now you are ready to LINK each chapter listed in the TOC to the place the chapter exists in the book.

Highlight the name of the first chapter. Use the Inert ribbon and select Hyperlink. In the dialogue window, select Place in this Document in the left hand panel. Now, find the bookmark that corresponds to the chapter, select it and press okay.

Do the same for all of the items in the Table of Contents.

When you have finished, use the same method for creating a bookmark named "TOC" above the title of the Table of Contents. (Remember to use an empty line).

There are a number of eBooks, websites and resources that describe processes similar to this. It helps if you select one with screen shots and prepared by someone with more experience than I have. An experienced professional will give better explanations of what to do if the process does not work when you set it up manually. I wanted to give you an overview and help you know what you were looking for when you look up how to create a table of contents. If you are detail oriented, patient and a little technically inclined the list of steps will result in a working TOC.

Disclaimer

Notification to Reader and Disclaimer

This jump-start guide is an initial sketch of ideas for anyone attempting to independently publish. The writer does not intend the information in this publication to be a complete how-to-manual. With this guide and a commitment to thorough research and seeking professional help, the reader should be able to learn enough to independently publish. There is no implied assurance of income or success.

DISCLAIMER:

The information included is for the purpose of giving examples. The resources mentioned will give the reader ideas about some providers of services or products. We do not endorse or recommend any particular products or services. We do not receive payment for the inclusion of any resource. The writer acknowledges that all trademarks, service marks and copyrighted information from the internet resources are the property of the legal owners. The writer has attempted to notify (electronically) the owner of each site that the writer listed the owner as an example in this publication. The reader is responsible for personal and business decisions related to the information and is encouraged to research any organization before entering into an agreement or paying for services or products.

The publisher and the author make no representations or warranties with respect to the accuracy or the completeness of the contents of this work. The opinions, information and ideas in this work may not be suitable for every situation. This work is sold with the understanding that neither the publisher nor the author are engaged in rendering any legal, accounting or other professional services in this publication. If professional assistance is required, the services of a competent professional should be sought. Neither the publisher nor the author shall be liable for damages. The fact that an article, book, website or organization is referred to in this work as a citation and/or a potential source of further information does not mean that the author or the publisher endorses the information. Readers should be aware that internet websites listed in this work may have changed between when this work was written and when it is read.

Trademark, Servicemarks, etc.

The trademarked and servicemarked companies mentioned in this book remain the legally protected mark of the company that owns the name, service or term. No affiliation is implied or exists. No monetary relationship exists other than the possibility of the author's own paid or unpaid use of some of the described services.

Resources

You may want to make notes from your research or include updates on these pages.

The worksheets, charts and some additional material related to this guide are available online from the publisher at:
http://tiny.cc/JSGIPBonus
Click through the prompts and register for the downloads.

www.ingramcontent.com/pod-product-compliance
Lightning Source LLC
Chambersburg PA
CBHW061034050326
40689CB00012B/2808